HISTORY FROM OBJECTS
CLOTHES

Karen Bryant-Mole

Wayland

HISTORY FROM OBJECTS

In The Home
Keeping Clean
At School
Toys
Clothes
In The Street

This edition published in 1996 by
Wayland (Publishers) Ltd

First published in 1994 by Wayland (Publishers) Ltd,
61 Western Road, Hove, East Sussex, BN3 1JD, England

Edited by Deborah Elliott
Designed by Malcolm Walker

British Library Cataloguing in Publication Data
Bryant-Mole, Karen
   Clothes. - (History From Objects Series)
   I. Title II. Series
   391.009

HARDBACK ISBN 0-7502-1019-2

PAPERBACK ISBN 0-7502-1894-0

Typeset by Kudos Editorial and Design Services
Printed and bound by BPC Paulton Books Ltd

Notes for parents and teachers
This book has been designed to be used on many different levels. It can be used as a means of comparing and contrasting clothes from the past with those of the present. Differences between the clothes can be identified.

It can be used to look at the way designs have developed as our knowledge and technology have improved. Children can consider the similarities between the clothes and look at the way particular design features have been refined. They can look at the materials that the clothes are made from. The book can be used to help place objects in chronological order and to help children understand that development in design corresponds with a progression through time.

It can also be used to make deductions about the way people in the past lived their lives. It is designed to show children that historical clothes can reveal much about the past. At the same time it links the past with the present by showing that many of the familiar clothes we wear today have their roots planted firmly in history.

Contents

Some of the more difficult words which appear in **bold** in the text are explained in the glossary on page 30.

Sports clothes

1910s

These women are going to play tennis in skirts which go down to their ankles and long-sleeved blouses. It must have been very difficult to run across the tennis court in such long skirts.

1950s

These tennis clothes are all white. The women's skirts come down to their knees. Can you see the difference between the sleeves on their shirts and those from the 1910s? It must have been easier and cooler to play tennis in short-sleeved shirts like these.

Now

Today, tennis skirts are very short. Men wear shorts to play tennis. This player is wearing special tennis shoes.

Swimming costumes

1900s

Most people did not own a swimming costume. When families visited the seaside they usually went for a paddle rather than a swim.

1920s

These swimming costumes are made up of a tunic and long knickers. The women would probably have changed their clothes in bathing huts on the beach. Do you like their swimming hats?

1950s

One of these women is wearing a bikini and the other is wearing a one-piece swimsuit. One woman is wearing a rubber swimming hat. These swimming costumes fitted more closely to the body.

Now

Some girls prefer swimsuits to bikinis. Very few people wear swimming hats these days. Most of today's swimming costumes are made from very stretchy material, such as elasticated nylon.

Rainwear

1960s

This boy's coat and hat are made from a material called gabardine. Gabardine is **woven** in a special way which makes water run off it.

1890s

In the 1890s, children often wore clothes that were small **versions** of adult's clothes. This waterproof coat, with a cape but no sleeves, was made in both boys' and mens' sizes.

Now

These children are wearing coats made from brightly coloured plastic.
They are holding a see-through umbrella over their heads. Plastic is a good material for rainwear because it is waterproof.

Dressing up

1910s

The children and adults in this picture are dressed up as pierrots, which are a type of clown. Pierrot groups used to travel to different villages, holding singing and dancing shows. Can you see a dog in a pierrot costume too?

1930s

This family is dressed up in costume. Perhaps everyone was going to a fancy-dress party, or a fancy-dress competition.

Now

These two children have dressed up in adults' clothes. They have put on some make-up too. Have you ever dressed up in adults' clothes?

Outdoor clothes

1910s

These girls are wearing coats or long jackets and hats with wide **brims**. Some of the girls are wearing two-piece suits. The skirts are all different lengths. Usually, older girls wore longer skirts.

1930s

The children are wearing coats which came down to their knees. The coats are done up with buttons. It must have been a very cold day because all the children are wearing hats or have scarves tied around their heads.

Now

Today, lots of people wear jackets rather than coats. Many of these jackets have zips down the front instead of buttons. Zips are much easier to do up. Some of these coats have hoods attached which means the children don't have to wear hats.

Uniforms

1900s

Nurses wore long white aprons over dresses which came down to their ankles.
The white **cuffs** could be taken off the dresses and washed separately.
These nurses wore hats tied on with big bows.

1930s

Although dresses and aprons were shorter, the style of nurse's uniform did not change for many years.

Now

This nurse is wearing a white dress with buttons down the front. The red belt means that she is a children's nurse. She has a watch pinned to her uniform. Can you see some pens and a pair of scissors in her pocket?

Wedding clothes

1890s

The bride's dress has an extra long piece of material at the back called a train. Most of the women guests are wearing tall, narrow hats. Lots of the guests are carrying **posies** of flowers.

1920s

This bride's dress has a long train too. She is also wearing a long veil. Her bridesmaids are all wearing dresses with short sleeves. The bride has short hair which was the popular way to have your hair in the 1920s.

1960s

The bride and her bridesmaid are both wearing mini dresses. Minis were very fashionable in the 1960s. The bride is wearing a white hair decoration instead of a veil.

Now

Today, many brides choose a **traditional** style of wedding dress rather than something which looks more modern. The men, and even the page boy, are wearing jackets with tails.

17

Summer clothes

1910s

The women are wearing long-sleeved clothes with skirts which come down to their ankles. Most are wearing wide-brimmed hats to shade their faces from the sun. The men are wearing suits and peaked caps or straw **boaters**.

1930s

The men in this picture are wearing **casual** trousers rather than suits. Only one man is wearing a tie. The women and girls are wearing short-sleeved cotton summer dresses.

Now

Many people today like to wear clothes that look sporty. T-shirts, shorts and training shoes or boots are very popular.

School clothes

1900s

These boys all had to wear the same type of clothes for school. Some of the boys in the front row are wearing long shorts, called knickerbockers.

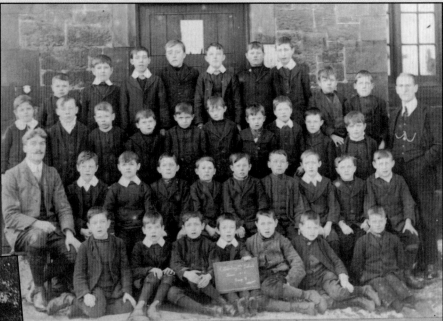

1920s

This school did not have a uniform. The woollen dresses and jumpers would probably have been knitted by hand. Can you see a boy in a sailor suit in the front row?

Now

This school uniform is comfortable to wear and easy to wash.
The children can choose between different sorts of clothes, but everyone wears a blue sweatshirt with the school's name on it. What do you wear to school?

Nightdresses

1900s

This long, white cotton nightdress has **ruffles** and lace on the cuffs, the collar and front. It is done up with buttons covered with **linen**. This loose style of nightdress was worn for many years.

1930s

Here are a woollen nightdress and dressing gown. You can see that the nightdress still has ruffles on the cuffs, collar and front, but it has more shape than the 1900s nightdress.

1960s
This is a very different style of nightdress, but you can see that ruffles and lace were still popular. This nightdress is made from a light, cotton material called lawn.

Now
Many people wear nightshirts in bed. These are like big T-shirts. They come with lots of different designs on them. This one has two teddies on the front.

23

Underwear

1920s

The stockings in the window are made from a material called rayon. Rayon looked like silk but was much cheaper. Women often wore camisoles under their dresses. These were like loose, shapeless vests.

1950s

Women's underwear was very tight fitting. It made their bodies look a certain shape. It must have been very uncomfortable to wear.

Now

Today's underwear is made to be comfortable to wear. Some of the underwear you can see in this shop looks a bit like the underwear from the 1920s.

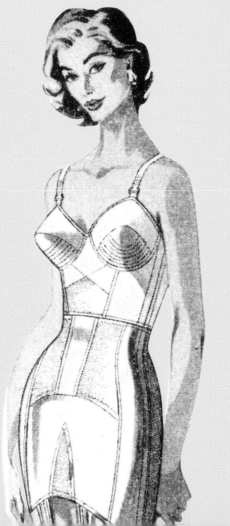

25

Boots and shoes

1900s

These high, buttoned boots came with or without shiny, **patent leather** toe caps. This style of heel was called a Louis heel.

The "**Prospero**"

Glace Kid.
Excellent Value.

BUTTON. SELF CAP.

WHEATSHEAF
Prospero
BRAND

8/11

The "**Prospero**"

Glace Kid.
Excellent Value.

BUTTON. PATENT CAP.

WHEATSHEAF
Prospero
BRAND

8/11

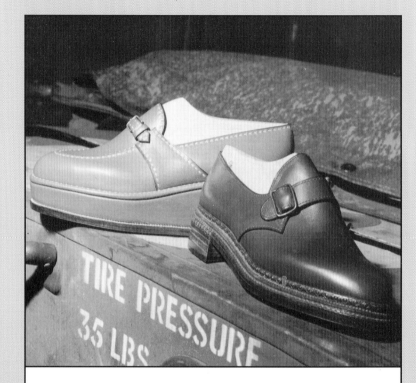

1940s

The light-coloured shoe has a built-up platform sole and a wedge-shaped heel. The dark-coloured shoe is called a monkskin. Both shoes have a buckle across the front.

1960s

Black and white were very popular colours at this time. Many boots and shoes had square toes and were often made from plastic.
The boots were just pulled on. The leg part of the boot was made from stretchy plastic.

Now

Today's shoes come in lots of different styles and colours.
Can you spot a boot, a red suede shoe, a trainer, a platform shoe and a brown lace-up shoe in this picture.

Best clothes

1910s

These two girls are wearing hats called tam o'shanters. Clothes based on traditional Scottish costume and material were often worn. The girls' dresses have lace collars and there is lace trimming on their skirts.

28

Now

The two girls are wearing party dresses with fitted velvet tops and gathered skirts. One girl has plain tights, and the other has patterned tights. Their shoes are made from shiny, patent leather.

1960s

This photograph was taken on the little girl's birthday. She is wearing a white dress with velvet spots. The dress was tied with a **sash**. She wore a stiff white petticoat under the dress to make it stick out.

Glossary

boaters   hard, straw hats

brims   the edges of hats

casual   everyday, not best clothes

cuffs   the bottom part of sleeves

linen   material made from flax, a bit like thick cotton

patent leather   leather that has been finished in a special way to make it very shiny

platform shoe   a shoe with a very large, thick heel

posies   small bunches of flowers carried by hand

ruffles   frills

sash   a strip of ribbon or cloth worn around the waist

traditional   the way things have been done for many years

versions   other ways of doing things

woven   the way in which threads have been put together to make cloth

Books to read

History From Photographs series by Kath Cox and Pat Hughes (Wayland, 1995-6)
How We Used To Live, 1902-1926 by Freda Kelsall (A & C Black, 1985)
How We Used To Live, 1954-1970 by Freda Kelsall (A & C Black, 1987)
Looking Back series (Wayland, 1991)
People Through History series by Karen Bryant-Mole (Wayland, 1996)
Starting History series (Wayland, 1991)

Index

Acknowledgements
The publishers would like to thank the following individuals and organizations, which supplied the photographs used in this book: APM Photographic 27 (bottom); Beamish, The North of England Open Air Museum 4, 5 (top), 6 (bottom), 8 (left), 10, 11 (left), 16 (both), 18, 19 (top), 20 (both), 24 (both), 25 (left), 26 (left), 28; Patricia Bryant 29 (left); Lynette Butler 17 (left); Camera Press 7 (right), 9; Cephas 25 (right, John Heinrich); Chapel Studios 13 (bottom), 15 (right), 21 (right), 22 (left), 23 (right), 27 (top), 29 (right); Lee Miller Archives 7 (left), 26 (right); Popperfoto 5 (bottom); Tony Stone Worldwide 11 (right, Myrleen Ferguson); Wayland Picture Library 19 (bottom) The photograph on page 17 (left) was taken by Sebastian Best, Beaminster. Shoes on page 27 (top) courtesy of Revamp, Brighton.